A Note From Rick Renner

I am on a personal quest to see a "revival of the Bible" so people can establish their lives on a firm foundation that will stand strong and endure the test as the end-time storm winds begin to intensify.

In order to experience a revival of the Bible in your personal life, it is important to take time each day to read, receive, and apply its truths to your life. James tells us that if we will continue in the perfect law of liberty — refusing to be forgetful hearers but determined to be doers — we will be blessed in our ways. As you watch or listen to the programs in this series and work through this corresponding study guide, I trust that you will search the Scriptures and allow the Holy Spirit to help you hear something new from God's Word that applies specifically to your life. I encourage you to be a doer of the Word that He reveals to you. Whatever the cost, I assure you — it will be worth it.

> Thy words were found, and I did eat them;
> and thy word was unto me the joy and rejoicing of mine heart:
> for I am called by thy name, O Lord God of hosts.
> — Jeremiah 15:16

Your brother and friend in Jesus Christ,

Rick Renner

Different Kinds of Prayer

Copyright © 2021 by Rick Renner
8316 E. 73rd St.
Tulsa, Oklahoma 74133

Published by Rick Renner Ministries
www.renner.org

ISBN 13: 978-1-68031-831-9

eBook ISBN 13: 978-1-68031-832-6

How To Use This Study Guide

This five-lesson study guide corresponds to *"Different Kinds of Prayer"* *With Rick Renner* (Renner TV). Each lesson in this study guide covers a topic that is addressed during the program series, with questions and references supplied to draw you deeper into your own private study of the Scriptures on this subject.

To derive the most benefit from this study guide, consider the following:

First, watch or listen to the program prior to working through the corresponding lesson in this guide. (Programs can also be viewed at **renner.org** by clicking on the Media/Archives links.)

Second, take the time to look up the scriptures included in each lesson. Prayerfully consider their application to your own life.

Third, use a journal or notebook to make note of your answers to each lesson's Study Questions and Practical Application challenges.

Fourth, invest specific time in prayer and in the Word of God to consult with the Holy Spirit. Write down the scriptures or insights He reveals to you.

Finally, take action! Whatever the Lord tells you to do according to His Word, do it.

For added insights on this subject, it is recommended that you obtain Germaine Copeland's book *Prayers That Avail Much: Scriptural Prayers for Your Daily Breakthrough*. You may also select from Rick Renner's available resources by placing your order at **renner.org** or by calling 1-800-742-5593.

TOPIC

Different Kinds of Prayer

SCRIPTURES

1. **Ephesians 6:18** — Praying always with all prayer and supplication in the Spirit, and watching thereunto with all perseverance and supplication for all saints.

GREEK WORDS

1. "with all prayer" — **διὰ πάσης προσευχῆς** (*dia pases proseuches*): with all kinds of prayer

2. "always" — **ἐν παντὶ καιρῷ** (*en panti kairo*): the word **ἐν** (*en*) would be better translated "at"; the word **παντὶ** (*panti*) means each and every, and it is an all-encompassing word that embraces everything, including the smallest and most minute of details; the word **καιρῷ** (*kairo*) is the Greek word for times or seasons; when used in one phrase as in Ephesians 6:18, it would be more accurately translated "at each and every occasion"

SYNOPSIS

The five lessons in this study on *Different Kinds of Prayer* will focus on the following topics:

- Different Kinds of Prayer
- Prayer of Consecration
- Prayer of Petition, Prayer of Authority
- Prayer of Thanksgiving, Prayer of Agreement
- Prayer of Supplication, Prayer of Intercession

The emphasis of this lesson:

One of the most often overlooked spiritual weapons we have been given as believers is the weapon of prayer. The Bible tells us that we are to pray without ceasing, using the different kinds of prayer God has provided.

As we abide in relationship with Him, the Holy Spirit will teach us which type of prayer we're to use in each and every situation we face.

In a typical toolbox, there are all kinds of tools to be used for all kinds of jobs. There are pliers for grabbing and pulling or bending things. There is a hammer for pounding nails in and pulling nails out. Then there's a wrench for tightening and loosening nuts, and of course there's a screwdriver to tighten screws in place. Each of these tools is very important and designed to perform a specific task.

In the same way, God has provided us with a spiritual toolbox in which we are given many different types of prayer that are each designed for a specific purpose. These include the *prayer of consecration*, the *prayer of petition*, and the *prayer of authority*, which some people call the *prayer of faith*. Then there is the *prayer of thanksgiving*, the *prayer of agreement*, the *prayer of supplication*, and the *prayer of intercession*. Each of these types of prayer is very important and serves a different purpose from each of the others. The fact that there are so many kinds of prayer lets us know that one size prayer does not fit all situations. When we use the right prayer at the right time, powerful things take place!

We Are To Pray
'With All Prayer'

Under the inspiration of the Holy Spirit, the apostle Paul described the whole armor of God in his letter to the church of Ephesus. And in Ephesians 6:18 he said we are to be "Praying always with all prayer and supplication in the Spirit, and watching thereunto with all perseverance and supplication for all saints." This verse is quite remarkable. It actually identifies the seventh major piece of the Roman soldier's armor, which is his *lance*. As believers, it is the final piece of the armor of God — "the lance of prayer and supplication."

Notice the words "with all prayer" in this verse. It is a translation of the Greek phrase *dia pases proseuches*, and it literally means *with all kinds of prayer*. Just as Roman soldiers had many different types of lances they used in battle, Paul tells us that God has made many kinds of prayer available to us for different moments in our fight of faith. Yes, it is true that our victory has already been won through Jesus' death and resurrection. But regardless of how skilled, bold, and courageous we think we are, when it comes to the issue of spiritual conflict, we simply cannot maintain a victorious position apart from a life of prayer. Without this vital spiritual weapon, we can be sure of defeat!

On the other hand, as we seek God in prayer to receive His direction and His power for our daily living, we get ourselves in position to victoriously reinforce Jesus Christ's triumphant victory over Satan and gloriously demonstrate Satan's miserable defeat. To assist us in maintaining this victorious position, God has given the Church various kinds of powerful prayer. Thus, the phrase "praying always with all prayer and supplication" can be translated:

"Pray with all manner of prayer."

"Pray with all kinds of prayer."

"Pray with all the kinds of prayers that are available for you to use."

Again, prayer is not a "one size fits all" weapon. There is a specific prayer for each specific event we face, and we need to learn how to pray in every situation we encounter.

Seven Kinds of Prayer for the Believer

The New Testament uses several different Greek words for prayer that are available for our use. Each one of these forms of prayer is different from the others and is symbolized by the multiple types of Roman lances that were used to battle against enemy forces. Each form of prayer is continually at our disposal to use in our fight of faith, and they can be categorized as:

1. **Prayer of Consecration** – The first type of prayer talked about all throughout the New Testament is the *prayer of consecration*. It is taken from a translation of the Greek word *proseuchomai*, which is the compound of the words *pros* and *euchomai*. The word *pros* denotes something that is *close* or *intimate*. This is very important because it tells us that prayer is intended to bring us into a place of divine intimacy.

   The second part of the word, the Greek word *euchomai*, is a derivative of the word *euche*, which is the word for *a vow* or *a commitment*. It pictures us coming to the alter drawing near to the Lord where we commit ourselves and pledge ourselves to God and ask Him to do something in our life. The compounded word *proseuchomai* — the *prayer of consecration* — is the number one most widely used word for prayer in the New Testament, appearing more than 127 times.

2. **Prayer of Petition** – The second type of prayer is called *the prayer of petition* and is derived from the Greek word *deesis*, which literally describes *a need* or *a want*. It appears in various forms and is used more than 40 times in the New Testament. It is the second most common word for prayer in Scripture.

3. **Prayer of Authority** (or the Prayer of Faith) – This third type of prayer is taken from the Greek word *aiteo*, and we find this word used approximately 80 times all over the New Testament. Jesus Himself used it in John 15:7 to describe asking God for something based on His Word abiding in our hearts. The word *aiteo* really means *to demand* or *to command* that something be done.

   The use of this word *aiteo* — describing the *prayer of authority* — tells us that when we know and are confident of what the Bible says, we don't have to be sheepish when we pray. We can be confident, bold, and frank. In fact, we can be so direct that we can nearly demand and command what needs to be done based on God's Word. Again, this is what Jesus encouraged us to do in John 15:7.

4. **Prayer of Thanksgiving** – The fourth kind of prayer talked about in Scripture is the *prayer of thanksgiving*. It is taken from the Greek word *eucharisteo*, which is a compound of the words *eu* and *charistia*. The word *eu* describes something that is *good* or *well*, and it denotes a general *good disposition* or *feeling* about someone or something.

   The second part of the word *eucharisteo* — the word *charistia* — is a form of the Greek word *charis*, which is the Greek word for *grace*. When *eu* and *charistia* are compounded, the new word *eucharisteo* refers to *wonderful feelings and good sentiments that freely flow up out of the heart in response to something*. The prayer of thanksgiving (*eucharisteo*) is seen all over the New Testament, especially in Paul's epistles where he joyfully *thanks* God for a certain person or group of people.

5. **Prayer of Supplication** – The fifth form of prayer found in the New Testament is the *prayer of supplication*, and it is taken from the Greek word *enteuxis*. It is a compound of the Greek words *en* and *tugchano*. The word *en* in this case means *in* or *into*; and the word *tugchano* means *to happen upon* or *to fall into*. When these words are compounded, it forms the Greek word *enteuxis*, which means *to fall into a situation* or *to happen into a circumstance* with someone else. It depicts us falling into a place of love with Jesus when we pray, and it is used only five times in the New Testament.

6. **Prayer of Agreement** – Another kind of prayer talked about in Scripture is what we would call the *prayer of agreement.* Jesus discussed this in Matthew 18:19 where He said, "Again I say unto you, that if two of you shall agree on earth as touching any thing that they shall ask, it shall be done for them of my Father which is in heaven."

   The word "agree" in this verse is the Greek word *sumphoneo,* which is where we get the word *symphony.* It means *to agree together* or *to come into agreement,* and it conveys the idea of *harmony* and *unity* in prayer. When we get into harmony with each other on any issue God has promised in His Word, He moves into action. That's what Jesus said here.

7. **Prayer of Intercession** – The seventh word for prayer used in the New Testament is taken from the long Greek word *huperentugchano.* It is the rarest of all the words denoting prayer and is only found one time in the entire New Testament. Furthermore, the place in Scripture where it is found is the first time it is ever used chronologically anywhere in Greek literature, which means it was created directly by the Holy Spirit just for Romans 8:26, and it denotes *supernatural prayer* or *intercession* by the Holy Spirit Himself.

How Often Should You Pray?

In addition to telling us we are to pray with all kinds of prayer, Paul also said we are to pray "always." This word "always" is a translation of the Greek phrase *en panti kairo,* which is a compound of three words: the words *en, panti,* and *kairo.* The word *en* would be better translated "at." The word *panti* means *each and every,* and it is an all-encompassing word that embraces *everything,* including *the smallest and most minute of details.* And the word *kairo* is the Greek word for *times* or *seasons.*

When these three words are compounded to form *en panti kairo* — translated here in Ephesians 6:18 as "always" — it would be more accurately translated "at each and every occasion" or "at every opportunity." Essentially, Paul is telling us, "Pray at each and every chance you get, regardless of where you are or what you are doing." This is the same truth we find in First Thessalonians 5:17, which says, "Pray without ceasing."

Now you may be thinking, *How can I pray without ceasing? Am I supposed to spend my every waking moment on my knees in prayer?* The answer is obviously no. You have a life to live, children to feed and raise, bills to pay, and other specific assignments God has given you to carry out. To "pray without ceasing" means to remain in an attitude of prayer all through the day — ready to pray anywhere about anything the Holy Spirit prompts you to pray about.

From the moment your eyes open in the morning, you can begin praying to the Father. Before your feet hit the floor, you can surrender yourself to His keeping and ask Him to use you as an instrument of righteousness. You can pray for your spouse, your children, your grandchildren, your friends, and your loved ones. As you get dressed and head into the kitchen for breakfast, you can invite the Lord to direct your every step that day and accomplish His divine will in and through your life. You can pray and give thanks for each meal as well as ask Him to open your mind and give you an understanding of the Scriptures as you read. You can pray while you're in the shower, in your car, or silently during a meeting at work.

Remember, God has given you all kinds of prayers to pray, and as you abide in relationship with Him, the Holy Spirit will teach you what type of prayer to use and when to use it. They are each a tool in your spiritual toolbox. In our next lesson, we'll take a more in-depth look at the *prayer of consecration*.

STUDY QUESTIONS

Study to shew thyself approved unto God, a workman that needeth not to be ashamed, rightly dividing the word of truth.
— 2 Timothy 2:15

1. Prior to this lesson, what did you understand prayer to be? Did you know that there were multiple forms of prayer?
2. Take a moment to list each of the seven different types of prayer found in the New Testament, and in your own words write a simple, one-sentence definition for each to help you remember them.
3. Of all the different kinds of prayer presented in this lesson, which one (ones) are you most familiar with and have used? Which kind of prayer are you least familiar with?
4. When you think about the subject of prayer, what Bible verses come to mind?

PRACTICAL APPLICATION

> But be ye doers of the word, and not hearers only,
> deceiving your own selves.
> — James 1:22

1. How would you describe *your* prayer life? Would you say it is *consistent* or *sporadic*? *Life-giving* or *exhausting*? Do you see prayer as a daily *duty* that needs to be done or a *privileged opportunity* to connect with your heavenly Father?

2. In your own words, explain what God means when He says to "pray without ceasing."

3. Given the challenges you're currently facing, what kind of prayer do you feel is most fitting to use at this time? Pause right now and pray over these situations that are weighing on your mind and emotions and do what Peter instructed in First Peter 5:7 (*AMPC*):

   "Casting the whole of your care [all your anxieties, all your worries, all your concerns, once and for all] on Him, for He cares for you affectionately and cares for you watchfully."

LESSON 2

TOPIC

Prayer of Consecration

SCRIPTURES

1. **Ephesians 6:18** — Praying always with all prayer and supplication in the Spirit, and watching thereunto with all perseverance and supplication for all saints.

2. **John 1:1** — In the beginning was the Word, and the Word was with God, and the Word was God.

3. **1 Samuel 1:10,11** — And she was in bitterness of soul, and prayed unto the Lord, and wept sore. And she vowed a vow, and said, O Lord of hosts, if thou wilt indeed look on the affliction of thine handmaid, and remember me, and not forget thine handmaid, but wilt give unto

thine handmaid a man child, then I will give him unto the Lord all the days of his life, and there shall no razor come upon his head.

4. **1 Samuel 1:19,20** — And they [Hannah and her husband, Elkanah] rose up in the morning early, and worshipped before the Lord, and returned, and came to their house in Ramah: and Elkanah knew Hannah his wife; and the Lord remembered her. Wherefore it came to pass, when the time was come about after Hannah had conceived, that she bare a son....

GREEK WORDS

1. "with all prayer" — διὰ πάσης προσευχῆς (*dia pases proseuches*): with all kinds of prayer

2. "prayer" — προσεύχομαι (*proseuchomai*): compound of πρός (*pros*) and εὔχομαι (*euchomai*); the word πρός (*pros*) means toward and implies closeness; the word εὔχομαι (*euchomai*) means to offer a request; compounded, to come near to offer a request

SYNOPSIS

As we saw in Lesson 1, the average toolbox is filled with a variety of different instruments, each one uniquely crafted to help fix a certain problem. Sometimes there is even diversity within a specific category of tool. Take for example a screwdriver. The most common screws have either a Philips head or a flat head, but there are also star-type and hex-head screws. Thus, there are multiple types of screwdrivers to use with each type of known screw.

In the same way, God has given us a spiritual toolbox, and in it there are various types of prayer, each serving a particular purpose. Over time and through the leading of the Holy Spirit, we learn to discern which type of prayer to use in each situation we face and the way we are to use it most effectively. The right type of prayer used at the right time produces the right results. One specific type of prayer we have been given is the *prayer of consecration*.

The emphasis of this lesson:

The most common type of prayer talked about in the New Testament is the prayer of consecration, from the Greek word *proseuchomai*. It tells us that prayer is a face-to-face encounter with God where we make a vow

and fully surrender our lives to Him in exchange for Him giving us His life and answering our request.

A Review of Our Anchor Verse

In our anchor verse for this series, the apostle Paul concludes his description of the armor of God by describing one of the most powerful weapons we have been given — *prayer*. He said we are to be "Praying always with all prayer and supplication in the Spirit, and watching thereunto with all perseverance and supplication for all saints" (Ephesians 6:18).

The phrase "with all prayer" is taken from the Greek words *dia pases proseuches*, which means *with all kinds of prayer*. This portion of Scripture could actually be translated "pray with all manner of prayer," "pray with all sorts of prayer," or "pray with all the kinds of prayers that are available for you to use." This clearly confirms that God has made many types of prayer available for us to utilize.

It is also important to note that we are instructed to pray "always." In Greek, the word "always" is the phrase *en panti kairo*, a compound of three words. The word *en* means *at*; the word *panti* means *each and every*, and it is an all-encompassing word that embraces *everything*, including *the smallest and most minute of details*. The third word *kairo* is the Greek word for *times* or *seasons*. When all three words are used in one phrase (*en panti kairo*) as in Ephesians 6:18, it would be more accurately rendered "at each and every occasion." It could also be translated to read:

"Pray at every opportunity."

"Pray every time you get a chance."

"Pray at every season."

"Pray at each and every possible moment."

The idea Paul is trying to get across to us is this:

> **"Anytime you get a chance, no matter where you are or what you are doing, at every opportunity, every season, and every possible moment — SEIZE that time to pray!"**

Although many people find it more exciting to talk about the shield of faith, the sword of the Spirit, or the breastplate of righteousness, the lance of prayer and supplication is equal in importance to these other pieces of armor and one of the most powerful pieces of spiritual weaponry the Body of Christ possesses.

Pray Without Ceasing

First Thessalonians 5:17 reaffirms what Paul wrote in Ephesians 6:18. It says, "Pray without ceasing." The words "without ceasing" in Greek mean *without interruption, without interval,* or *without taking a break.* It describes something that happens *continuously, uninterruptedly, always,* or *persistently.* As we noted in the first lesson, this verse does *not* mean that we stay on our knees 24 hours a day. It is simply telling us to remain in an attitude of prayer everywhere we go and in everything we do. Therefore, in addition to having a concentrated time of prayer each day — which could be 30 seconds, 30 minutes, or longer — you should aim to maintain an attitude of prayer…

- From the moment you wake up in the morning.
- While you take care of things around your house.
- When you sit down to read God's Word.
- As you drive to and from your job.
- When you are at work or out in public.
- As you lay in bed preparing to go to sleep.

King David understood the power and importance of prayer. He declared, "Give ear to my words, O Lord, consider my meditation. Harken unto the voice of my cry, my King, and my God: for unto thee will I pray. My voice shalt thou hear in the morning, O Lord; in the morning will I direct my prayer unto thee, and will look up" (Psalm 5:1-3).

The truth is, God wants to be involved in everything that concerns you. The Bible says, "…The Spirit Whom He [God] has caused to dwell in us yearns over us and He yearns for the Spirit [to be welcome] with a jealous love" (James 4:5 *AMPC*). Whether you're taking the dog for a walk, taking out the trash, or making major decisions for you and your family, it is in your best interest to invite the Spirit of God into every single aspect of your life.

The Most Common Type of Prayer:
The Prayer of Consecration

As we learned in our first lesson, the Bible talks about several different kinds of prayer. These include the *prayer of consecration*, the *prayer of petition*, the *prayer of authority*, the *prayer of thanksgiving*, the *prayer of agreement*, the *prayer of supplication*, and the *prayer of intercession*. All of these types of prayer are spiritual tools in our toolbox.

The most common word for "prayer" in the New Testament is taken from the Greek word *proseuchomai*, and it refers to the *prayer of consecration*. This particular word in its various forms is used approximately 127 times in the New Testament. The fact that this word is used so frequently tells us that the Holy Spirit is declaring that the prayer of consecration is extremely important.

Paul uses the word *proseuchomai* in Ephesians 6:18, when he says, "Praying always with all prayer...." In both instances, the words "praying" and "prayer" are taken from the Greek word *proseuchomai*. This word is a compound of the words *pros* and *euchomai*. The word *pros* means *toward* and implies *closeness*; the word *euchomai* means *to offer a request*. When compounded to form *proseuchomai*, it means *to come near to offer a request*.

Prayer Is an Intimate Encounter With God

When we take a closer look at the word *pros* — the first part of the word *proseuchomai* — we see that it is the foundation of this word, and it is a preposition that means *face to face* or *eyeball to eyeball*. It is actually the very word used in John 1:1 to describe the relationship between Jesus and the Father. It says, "In the beginning was the Word, and the Word was with God, and the Word was God." The word "with" in this verse is taken from the Greek word *pros*.

By using this word to describe the relationship between the Father and the Son, the Holy Spirit is telling us that theirs is an *intimate* relationship. One translator has translated John 1:1, "In the beginning was the Word, and the Word was *face to face* with God...." It is a picture of such close intimacy that God the Father and Jesus His Son could nearly feel each other's breath breathing upon each other's face.

This word *pros* is also used in Ephesians 6:12 to picture our close contact with unseen, demonic spirits that have been marshaled against us. The apostle Paul writes, "For we wrestle not against flesh and blood, but against principalities, against powers, against the rulers of the darkness of this world, against spiritual wickedness in high places."

In this passage, the word "against" is seen five times, and in each incidence, it is the Greek word *pros*. Thus, the verse could be translated, "For we don't wrestle face to face with flesh and blood, but face to face with principalities, eyeball to eyeball with powers, ribcage to ribcage with the rulers of the darkness of this world, and face to face with spiritual wickedness in high places." It is because of this close, intimate contact with diabolical forces that we are instructed to "Put on the whole armour of God..." (Ephesians 6:11).

Nearly everywhere the word *pros* is used in the New Testament, it carries the meaning of *a close, up-front, intimate contact* with someone else. And when it is used in connection with prayer, it means God is calling us to a place of face-to-face intimacy with Him!

Prayer Often Includes a Vow or Promise

The second part of the word *proseuchomai* is derived from the Greek word *euche*, which is an old Greek word that describes a *wish, desire, prayer*, or *vow*. The word *euche* was originally used to depict a person who made some kind of vow to God because of a need or desire in his or her life. This individual would come to an altar, and instead of offering the sacrifice of an animal, they would *vow* to give something of great value to God in exchange for a favorable answer to prayer. A perfect example of this can be found in the story of Hannah, the mother of Samuel.

Hannah deeply desired a child but was not able to become pregnant. After being barren year after year, she cried out to God in great desperation and anguish of spirit. On one of her family's annual trips to worship and sacrifice to the Lord in Shiloh, the Bible says:

> And she [Hannah] was in bitterness of soul, and prayed unto the Lord, and wept sore. And she vowed a vow, and said, O Lord of hosts, if thou wilt indeed look on the affliction of thine handmaid, and remember me, and not forget thine handmaid, but wilt give unto thine handmaid a man child, then I will give

**him unto the Lord all the days of his life, and there shall no
razor come upon his head.**

1 Samuel 1:10,11

Note, Hannah prayed and made a solemn vow to the Lord. She said,
"Lord, if you answer my prayer and give me a son, I will give him back to
You to serve You all the days of his life." This is a vivid picture of the word
proseuchomai. How did God respond to Hannah's prayer? We see it just a
few verses later:

**And they [Hannah and her husband, Elkanah] rose up in the
morning early, and worshipped before the Lord, and returned,
and came to their house to Ramah: and Elkanah knew Hannah
his wife; and the Lord remembered her. Wherefore it came to
pass, when the time was come about after Hannah had conceived, that she bare a son, and called his name Samuel, saying
Because I have asked him of the Lord.**

1 Samuel 1:19,20

Quite frequently, people like Hannah who were seeking an answer to
prayer would offer God a gift of thanksgiving in advance. This was their
way of releasing their faith in the goodness of God and of thanking Him
for His favorable response to their prayer requests. Such offerings of praise
and thanksgiving were called "votive offerings" (derived from the word
"vow"). This votive offering was similar to a pledge, for it was the person's
promise that once his or her prayer was answered, they would be back to
give additional thanksgiving to God.

The Prayer of Consecration
Brings Us to an Altar of Great Exchange

Keep in mind that the majority of Paul's readers were Greek in origin,
so when they saw the Greek word *proseuchomai*, they understood the
full ramifications of what was being said. They knew that prayer was
something that would bring them face to face and intimately close (*pros*)
to God. They also realized that prayer would bring them to an altar where
they would make a divine exchange — they would consecrate and fully
yield themselves to God, and He would respond by answering their
request and providing them with what they need.

Because the word *proseuchomai* has to do with these concepts of *surrender* and *sacrifice*, this tells us that God obviously desires to do more than merely bless us. He wants to change us! Although the Holy Spirit may convict our hearts of areas that need to be surrendered to His sanctifying power, He will never forcibly take these things from us. Thus, this particular word for *prayer* points to a place of decision and consecration — an altar where we freely vow to give our lives to God in exchange for His life.

That said, the prayer of consecration (*proseuchomai*) is a place where we give God what we are — all our weaknesses, our defects, and our problems, as well as our talents, gifts, and skills. In exchange, He gives us His power, His presence, and all the goodness He is. What an amazing deal He offers!

Friend, through the use of this word *proseuchomai* — the most common word for "prayer" in the entire New Testament — God is telling you 127 times to come face to face with Him at the altar and surrender your life in exchange for His, consecrating yourself on an ongoing basis. Be sure to thank Him in advance for moving in your life.

In our next lesson, we will focus on two more types of prayer God has given us: the *prayer of petition* and the *prayer of authority*.

STUDY QUESTIONS

**Study to shew thyself approved unto God, a workman that needeth
not to be ashamed, rightly dividing the word of truth.
— 2 Timothy 2:15**

1. The Greek word *pros* is the first half of the word *proseuchomai*, which describes the prayer of consecration, and it means *a close, up-front, intimate contact* with someone else. What does this say to you personally about your prayer time with God?

2. In Ephesians 3:14-19, the apostle Paul prayed for the believers at Ephesus — and all believers throughout all generations — that we would come to personally and intimately know God. As you reflect on this passage, what is the Holy Spirit speaking to you through Paul's prayer? (Also consider Paul's words in Ephesians 1:15-19.)

PRACTICAL APPLICATION

**But be ye doers of the word, and not hearers only,
deceiving your own selves.
— James 1:22**

1. The second part of the word *proseuchomai* is derived from the word *euche*, which is an old Greek word that describes a *wish, desire, prayer,* or *vow.* Can you think of a time when you made a vow to God in order for Him to answer your prayer? What vow or promise did you make, and what were you asking Him to do for you in exchange?

2. Did He answer your prayer? If so, how? And were you faithful to fulfill the vow or pledge you made to God?

3. Be honest. When was the last time you came to the altar to meet with God face to face and surrender your life in exchange for His? Why not take time right now to give Him all your weaknesses, your defects, and your problems, as well as your talents, gifts, and skills. As you surrender all that you are to God, ask Him to give you all that He is — including His power, His presence, and all of His goodness.

LESSON 3

TOPIC

Prayer of Petition, Prayer of Authority

SCRIPTURES

1. **Ephesians 6:18** — Praying always with all prayer and supplication in the Spirit, and watching thereunto with all perseverance and supplication for all saints.

2. **Hebrews 5:7** — Who in the days of his flesh, when he had offered up prayers and supplications with strong crying and tears unto him that was able to save him from death, and was heard in that he feared.

3. **John 15:7** — If ye abide in me, and my words abide in you, ye shall ask what ye will, and it shall be done unto you.

4. **Hebrews 4:16** — Let us therefore come boldly unto the throne of grace, that we may obtain mercy, and find grace to help in time of need.

5. **1 John 5:14,15** — And this is the confidence that we have in him, that, if we ask any thing according to his will, he heareth us: and if we know that he hear us, whatsoever we ask, we know that we have the petitions that we desired of him.

GREEK WORDS

1. "with all prayer" — διὰ πάσης προσευχῆς (*dia pases proseuches*): with all kinds of prayer

2. "supplication" — δέησις (*deesis*): its various forms are translated prayer and petition more than 40 times in the New Testament

3. "pray" or "ask" — αἰτέω (*aiteo*): I ask or I demand; used approximately 80 times in the New Testament, making it the third most common word for prayer

4. "abide" — μένω (*meno*): stay, dwell, lodge, remain, continue

5. "confidence" — παρρησία (*parresia*): depicts someone who is exceedingly bold or courageous

6. "ask" — αἰτέω (*aiteo*): I ask or I demand; used approximately 80 times in the New Testament, making it the third most common word for prayer

SYNOPSIS

What do you think would happen if you tried to use a pair of pliers to pound in a nail — or tried to use a hammer to tighten a screw or a wrench to bend a piece of metal? Although each of these instruments is valuable and important, they are not the same instrument and cannot be used interchangeably. Each tool is designed to do a specific task and accomplish it effectively.

Similarly, God has given us various types of prayer, and each one is a valuable tool to accomplish a specific purpose. Paul talks about this in Ephesians 6:18 where he said we are to pray "…always with all prayer and supplication…."The phrase "with all prayer" means *all kinds of prayer*. It could also be translated to pray *with all manner of prayer* or *with all sorts of prayer*. Basically, it is Paul's way of saying, "Pray with all the kinds of prayer that are available for you to use."

The different kinds of prayer mentioned throughout the New Testament include:

1. The **prayer of consecration**, taken from the word *proseuchomai*
2. The **prayer of petition**, taken from the word *deesis*
3. The **prayer of authority**, taken from the word *aiteo*
4. The **prayer of agreement**, taken from the word *sumphoneo*
5. The **prayer of thanksgiving**, taken from the word *eucharisteo*
6. The **prayer of supplication**, taken from the word *enteuxis*
7. The **prayer of intercession**, taken from the word *huperentugchano*

The emphasis of this lesson:

The prayer of petition is an urgent cry for God's help, exposing our total dependence on Him to meet our needs. The prayer of authority is a bold demand for God to meet our needs, and it's based on the wealth of His Word stored up in our heart. The more that your mind is renewed to God's Word, the more your prayers will be in accordance with His plan for your life.

The Prayer of Petition

Looking once more at Paul's writing in Ephesians 6:18, he said, "Praying always with all prayer and supplication…." In this verse, the word "supplication" is the Greek word *deesis*, and it is the second most often used word for "prayer" in the New Testament, appearing more than 40 times and usually translated as *prayer* or *petition*.

This word *deesis* is taken from the verb *deomai*, which most literally describes *a need* or *a want*. It is the picture of a person with some kind of urgent need or desire in his or her personal life. As time passed, the word "need" began to take on the meaning of prayer — the kind of prayer that expresses one's basic needs and wants to God.

This word, however, has to do with very basic needs, not desires for tangible things such as larger homes, more expensive cars, etc. Rather, the word *deesis* has to do with the essential needs that must be met in order for a person to continue in his or her existence. You could therefore say that a *deesis* (prayer) is a *petition* or a cry for God's help that exposes a person's insufficiency to meet his or her own needs.

We find that Jesus prayed in this urgent manner, and it's recorded in Hebrews 5:7, which says,

> **Who in the days of his flesh, when he had offered up prayers and supplications with strong crying and tears unto him that was able to save him from death, and was heard in that he feared.**

The word "prayers" in this verse is taken from the Greek word *deesis*, which plainly tells us that Jesus recognized the insufficiency in His humanity to carry out the Father's plan of redemption. Therefore, He prayed (*deesis*) deeply from His heart and soul, asking the Father to move in His life at that moment and give Him the supernatural strength to endure the scourging and the crucifixion that was ahead of Him.

The word *deesis* — translated here as "prayers" — almost always portrays a faith-filled cry for help. A person praying this kind of prayer appeals to God from a position of humility as he or she asks God to grant some kind of special petition — such as a request for spiritual power to minister, for strength to resist temptation, or to be sustained in a crisis, etc.

Whereas the prayer of consecration — from the Greek word *proseuchomai* — has to do primarily with surrender and consecration, the prayer of petition (*deesis*) has to do with humility. Again, this word paints the picture of a believer who recognizes his utter dependence on God, and, therefore, his inability to meet his own need. Relying completely on God's ability to meet his need — whether it be spiritual, mental, or emotional — this person prays earnestly and sincerely, beseeching God from the depths of his spirit and soul to graciously move on his behalf.

The King James Version of Ephesians 6:18 says, "Praying always with all prayer and supplication [*deesis*]...." A better rendering would be, "Praying always, with all prayer and with all earnest, sincere, and heartfelt petitions."

The Prayer of Authority

The third form of prayer used in the New Testament is what we call the *prayer of authority*, and it is taken from the Greek word *aiteo*. A perfect example of this type of prayer is found in John 15:7, where Jesus said, "If ye abide in me, and my words abide in you, ye shall ask what ye will, and it shall be done unto you." In this verse, the word "ask" is the Greek word *aiteo*, and it means *to ask* or *to demand*, and it is used approximately 80 times in the New Testament.

At first glance, the word *aiteo* seems to be a strange word for "prayer" because it doesn't refer to one who humbly requests something from God. Rather, it describes someone who prays authoritatively, almost demanding something from God! This person knows what he needs, and he isn't afraid to boldly ask to receive it!

Unlike the word *deesis*, which has more to do with spiritual needs and wants, the word *aiteo* primarily has to do with *tangible needs*, such as food, shelter, money, and so forth. But how can one approach God with such frankness, commanding and demanding that his needs be met by God?

Jesus gave us the key to understanding this word *aiteo* in John 15:7. When He said, "…Ye shall ask what ye will, and it shall be done unto you," a better translation would be, "Ye shall *demand* what ye will, and it shall be done unto you." Although this notion of "demanding" something from God may seem disturbing, it begins to make sense when we interpret it in the context of the entire verse.

In the first part of John 15:7, Jesus said, "If ye abide in me, and my words abide in you…." The word "abide" here is the Greek word *meno*, which means *to stay, dwell, lodge, remain,* or *continue.* In light of this definition, you could translate the verse:

If you permanently and habitually lodge, abide, and remain continually in Me, and if My words permanently and habitually lodge, abide, and remain continually in you, you will be able to strongly ask for whatever you wish and it will be done for you.

The Lord knew if His words took up permanent residency in our hearts and minds, we would never ask for something that was out of line with His will for our lives. Hence, when we allow the Word of God to permanently and habitually lodge in our hearts, that Word so transforms our minds that when we pray, we do so in accordance with God's will.

It's Appropriate To Pray Boldly When God's Word Has Its Home in You

Friend, the great news is, when you know you're praying according to the will of God, you don't have to sheepishly utter your requests. Instead, you can boldly assert your faith and expect God to move on your behalf! This is why the writer of Hebrews says, "Let us therefore come boldly unto the throne of grace, that we may obtain mercy, and find grace to help in time of need" (Hebrews 4:16).

The apostle John echoes this principle and builds on it in First John 5:14 and 15:

> **And this is the confidence that we have in him, that, if we ask any thing according to his will, he heareth us: and if we know that he hear us, whatsoever we ask, we know that we have the petitions that we desired of him.**

Notice the word "confidence" in verse 14. It is the Greek word *parresia*, and it depicts *someone who is exceedingly bold or very courageous.* When you know you're speaking from the reservoir of God's Word abiding inside you and you're in agreement with that Word, you don't have to be sheepish when you pray. You can boldly pray an authoritative prayer.

John said we have this confidence "…if we ask any thing according to his will, he heareth us: and if we know that he hear us, whatsoever we ask, we know that we have the petitions that we desired of him." (1 John 5:14,15). Look again at the words "ask," "petitions," and "desired." All three of these words are taken from the same Greek word — the word *aiteo*, which means *to ask* or *to demand.* It is the same word used approximately 80 times in the New Testament.

Like Jesus' words in John 15:7, this passage tells us that if God's Word dwells in us, we can pray in accordance with His Word, and we do not need to be sheepish when we pray. For example, if your spouse is sick, you don't need to timidly ask God to heal them. You know from His Word it's His will to heal and therefore, you can demand and command that God heal them, and you can pray boldly with confidence expecting God to move. This is the prayer of authority.

God Wants You To Seize His Will for Your Life

To be clear, God is NOT offended by this type of outspoken prayer. If His Word dwells in you — if the Scriptures have lodged in your heart and mind and have taken up residency in your life — then you will not pray prayers that are out of line with God's plan. Thus, when you pray, your prayers will be accurate and in line with His predetermined plan for your life. You will be praying God's will!

When you have stored in your heart a strong foundation of accurate knowledge based in God's Word, you can be very bold and courageous in your prayer life, which is exactly what God wants you to do. His desire is that you move forward boldly and courageously in prayer in order to seize His will for your life and bring it into manifestation!

By allowing God's Word to take an authoritative role in your heart and mind, you are giving that Word the freedom to transform your thinking. And the more that your mind is renewed to God's Word, the more your prayers will be in accordance with His plan for your life. With the prayer of authority *(aiteo)* at your disposal, you can boldly, courageously, and confidently move into higher realms of prayer to obtain the petition you desire of God!

In our next lesson, we will explore the prayer of thanksgiving and the prayer of agreement.

STUDY QUESTIONS

Study to shew thyself approved unto God, a workman that needeth not to be ashamed, rightly dividing the word of truth.
— 2 Timothy 2:15

1. The *prayer of authority* is taken from the Greek word *aiteo*, which primarily has to do with *tangible needs*, such as food, shelter, money, and so forth. What did Jesus Himself say about Him meeting these needs in Matthew 6:25-34 (also in Luke 12:22-31)?

2. The key to effectively praying the *prayer of authority* (*aiteo*) is permanently abiding and remaining in relationship with Jesus and allowing His Word to permanently abide and remain in you. Read Colossians 3:16; Psalm 119:11; and Deuteronomy 6:6 and 11:18 to identify the importance of God's Word in your life.

3. When you take in the Word of God, you take in Jesus Himself because He is the Word (*see* John 1:1). According to the following passages, what are some of the wonderful effects you can expect to experience in your life when you regularly soak in the Scriptures?

   • **Romans 1:16**

   • **Proverbs 4:20-22**

   • **Hebrews 4:12**

- **James 1:21**
- **Jeremiah 5:14 and 23:29**
- **Acts 20:32**

PRACTICAL APPLICATION

> But be ye doers of the word, and not hearers only,
> deceiving your own selves.
> —James 1:22

1. The kind of attitude you have when you approach God in prayer is extremely important. Although He wants us to boldly and fearlessly come before His throne, He also wants us to show *respect* and *gratitude* for the privilege. How has your attitude been when you approach God in prayer? Have you been humble and respectful or have you unknowingly picked up a prideful attitude of entitlement? Is there anything you need to repent of? (Consider James 4:6 and First Peter 5:5 as you answer.)

2. The *prayer of petition* — from the Greek word *deesis* — has to do with one's very basic needs that must be met in order for them to continue in his or her existence. This petition is a deep, heartfelt request for strength to resist temptation, for spiritual power to minister, or to be sustained in a crisis. What urgent situation (or situations) are you facing that requires this kind of supernatural empowerment? Take time now to pray and ask God for His help.

LESSON 4

TOPIC

Prayer of Thanksgiving, Prayer of Agreement

SCRIPTURES

1. **Ephesians 6:18** — Praying always with all prayer and supplication in the Spirit, and watching thereunto with all perseverance and supplication for all saints.

2. **Ephesians 1:16** — [I] cease not to give thanks for you, making mention of you in my prayers.

3. **Colossians 1:3** — We give thanks to God and the Father of our Lord Jesus Christ, praying always for you.

4. **1 Thessalonians 1:2** — We give thanks to God always for you all, making mention of you in our prayers.

5. **1 Thessalonians 5:18** — In every thing give thanks: for this is the will of God in Christ Jesus concerning you.

GREEK WORDS

1. "with all prayer" — διὰ πάσης προσευχῆς (*dia pases proseuches*): with all kinds of prayer

2. "give thanks" — εὐχαριστέω (*eucharisteo*): compound of the words (*eu*) and (*charistia*); the word (*eu*) describes something that is good or well and denotes a general good disposition or feeling about something; the word (*charistia*) is from the word (*charis*), the word for grace; compounded, (*eucharistia*) refers to wonderful feelings and good sentiments that freely flow up out of the heart in response to something

3. "supplication" — ἔντευξις (*enteuxis*): taken from the root ἐντυγχάνω (*entugchano*) which is a compound of the word ἐν (*en*) and τυγχάνω (*tugchano*); the word ἐν (*en*) means in or into; the word τυγχάνω (*tugchano*); means to happen upon; compounded, it means to fall into a situation or to happen into a circumstance with someone else; but the word ἔντευξις (*enteuxis*) and its various forms are used only five times in the New Testament

SYNOPSIS

There is an interesting verse in Luke's gospel that says, "One day Jesus was praying in a certain place. When he finished, one of his disciples said to him, 'Lord, teach us to pray...'" (Luke 11:1 *NIV*). It appears that since the birth of Christianity, Christ's followers have wanted to know how to pray.

Thankfully, God's Word is filled with insights on the subject of prayer, including Ephesians 6:18 where Paul writes that we are to be, "Praying always with all prayer and supplication in the Spirit, and watching thereunto with all perseverance and supplication for all saints." We've seen in our previous lessons that the phrase "with all prayer" in Greek is *dia pases proseuches*, and it means *with all kinds of prayer*.

Just as there were a variety of lances used by Roman soldiers, God has supplied us with multiple kinds of prayer to use in our daily lives. One way of praying does not fit all circumstances and situations. But as we learn about the different kinds of prayer available to us and how to use the right prayer at the right time, we will experience great results.

The emphasis of this lesson:

Another prayer included in the New Testament is the prayer of thanksgiving, and it refers to wonderful feelings and good sentiments that freely flow up out of our hearts in response to something or someone. Additionally, we have been given the prayer of agreement, which is a harmonizing prayer between two or more believers that deeply touches the Father's heart and releases His power into our lives and our situations.

The Kinds of Prayer We've Studied Thus Far

In Lesson 2, we looked at the ***prayer of consecration***, which is taken from the Greek word *proseuchomai*. It is a compound of the word *pros*, which indicates *closeness* or *intimacy*, and a form of the word *euche*, which carries the idea of *a commitment, a pledge*, or *a vow*. When these two words are put together, the new word *proseuchomai* depicts a person who comes face to face (*pros*) with God in order to make a pledge or a vow and receive something he needs. It is a divine exchange.

This word *proseuchomai* — which we call the *prayer of consecration* — is the most frequently used word for *prayer* anywhere in the New Testament, appearing 127 times. The high frequency of this word tells us that God is calling us to the altar to come close to Him (*pros*) and to (*euchomai*) make a vow or a pledge to surrender our lives to Him in exchange for His life.

In Lesson 3, we examined the ***prayer of petition***, which is a translation of the Greek word *deesis*. It describes one who feels he has an urgent need in his life, a need that only God can fill. The *prayer of petition* (*deesis*) has to do with humility and paints the picture of a believer who recognizes his utter dependence on God, and, therefore, his inability to meet his own need. Whether it be a spiritual, mental, or emotional need, this person prays earnestly and sincerely, beseeching God from the depths of his spirit and soul to graciously move on his behalf.

We also explored the **prayer of authority** in our third lesson, which some call the *prayer of faith*. It is derived from the Greek word *aiteo*, a word used more than 80 times in the New Testament, and it means *to ask* or *to demand* something. When we allow the Word of God to permanently and habitually lodge in our hearts, that Word so transforms our minds that when we pray, we do so in accordance with God's will. Thus, the key to praying the prayer of authority is to have a strong foundation of accurate knowledge based in God's Word. In this position, you can be very bold and courageous in your prayer life, which is exactly what God wants you to do.

The Prayer of Thanksgiving

The fourth most common form of prayer in the New Testament is the *prayer of thanksgiving*, and it is taken from the Greek word *eucharisteo*. This word is used 15 times in various forms throughout the New Testament. It is primarily employed in Paul's epistles when he joyfully *gives thanks* to God for someone or for a group of individuals. For instance, when Paul wrote to the church at Ephesus, he was so amazed with the grace of God working in their midst that he spoke freely from the depths of his heart, saying:

> **[I] cease not to give thanks for you, making mention of you in my prayers.**
>
> **Ephesians 1:16**

In this verse, the words "give thanks" are a translation of the Greek word *eucharisteo*. It is a compound of the word *eu*, which describes something that is *good* or *well* and denotes *a general good disposition or feeling* about something; and the word *charistia*, which is from the word *charis*, the word for *grace*. When the words *eu* and *charistia* are compounded to form *eucharisteo*, it refers to *wonderful feelings and good sentiments that freely flow up out of the heart in response to something or someone*. This is a picture of one who feels something so profound, something so wonderful, that he can't contain what he feels and it just flows out of his heart like a river — a river of thanksgiving (*eucharisteo*).

The apostle Paul said the same thing when he addressed the believers in the church at Colossae:

We give thanks to God and the Father of our Lord Jesus Christ, praying always for you.

Colossians 1:3

Again, the words "give thanks" are a translation of the Greek word *eucharisteo*. These words by Paul are the equivalent of him saying, "My feelings concerning you cannot be contained. I cannot put a lid on the river of wonderful feelings and good sentiments that are freely flowing up out of my heart like a river. I just can't help but thank God for you!"

We see this exact same sentiment again in Paul's letter to the believers at the church in Thessalonica:

We give thanks to God always for you all, making mention of you in our prayers.

1 Thessalonians 1:2

Once more, we see the Greek word *eucharisteo* translated as "give thanks." Again and again, we see that Paul could not contain the overwhelming appreciation he had welling up in his heart for what the grace of God was doing in the lives of believers. Sure, these people had issues that needed to be corrected. But before Paul began to deal with the things they were doing wrong, he made it a point to first stop and think about everything good in their lives — a practice we, too, should adopt in our relationship with others, which is basically what Paul instructs us to do in First Thessalonians 5:18:

In every thing give thanks: for this is the will of God in Christ Jesus concerning you.

Yet again, we see the use of the Greek word *eucharisteo* translated here as "give thanks." In this verse, the Greek could better be rendered to read, "On every occasion and in every way possible give thanks." According to this verse, it is God's will that we use the prayer of thanksgiving in every aspect of our lives — especially when we're praying for others.

This means you should stop for a moment and reflect on all God has done in those individuals' lives. As you do, you will probably realize that, although they may still have flaws that are disturbing to you, they have made great progress from where they used to be. That should serve as a reminder of just how amazing and powerful God's grace is! This will enable you to freely, joyfully, and unreservedly thank God for His transforming work in their lives.

The Prayer of Agreement

There is another specific form of prayer God has entrusted to us, and it is the *prayer of agreement*. Jesus Himself discusses the power of this prayer in Matthew 18:19:

> **Again I say unto you, that if two of you shall agree on earth as touching any thing that they shall ask, it shall be done for them of my Father which is in heaven.**

Notice the word "agree" in this verse. It's the Greek word *sumphoneo*, which is where we get the word *symphony*. It is a compound of the word *sum*, which means *with*, and the word *phoneo*, which means *to make sound*. When these two words are combined to form *sumphoneo*, it describes *a harmonizing prayer among two or more believers*. Thus, when we come together in a prayer of agreement, it is like an orchestra of musicians coming together — each cooperating and playing their individual parts — uniting in a concert of prayer. This creates a supernatural movement that deeply touches the heart of the Father, and the result is Him answering and fulfilling the issue brought before Him.

It's important to grasp what Jesus is saying in this passage (Matthew 18:19). He is literally telling all believers — including *you* — that when we agree or symphonize together in prayer, it puts us in a powerful position that God will begin to move into action and do whatever we're asking Him to do.

There is a remarkable example of the prayer of agreement in Acts 4. In this passage, the Bible records that when Peter and John had been released from the custody of the Jewish officials, they came together in an upper room in Jerusalem and shared with fellow believers about how they were persecuted and brought before the chief priests and elders. "And when they [all the believers that were gathered] heard that, they lifted up their voice to God with one accord…" (Acts 4:24).

The phrase "with one accord" is a picture of a symphony (*sumphoneo*) of prayer. These First-Century believers began to pray in harmony with one another, lifting up their voices to God together in agreement. It was a moment of great unity. What was the result? Acts 4:31 says, "And when they had prayed, the place was shaken where they were assembled together; and they were all filled with the Holy Ghost, and they spake the word of God with boldness."

When the prayer of agreement was implemented, God moved mightily. Friend, when you and someone else come together in a prayer of agreement — both believing and declaring what God's Word says — great things take place! So learning how to play your part and harmonize with other believers in a symphony of prayer is extremely important.

In our final lesson, we'll take a closer look at two more kinds of prayer — the *prayer of supplication* and the *prayer of intercession*.

STUDY QUESTIONS

Study to shew thyself approved unto God, a workman that needeth not to be ashamed, rightly dividing the word of truth.
— 2 Timothy 2:15

1. How important do you think it is in God's eyes to be thankful and actually express it in your prayers? Read the following verses of Scripture and identify the priority He places on thankfulness.

   • Psalm 50:14,15; 92:1; 100:4

   • 1 Thessalonians 5:18

   • Ephesians 5:19,20

   • Philippians 4:6,7

2. Oftentimes instead of being thankful, the first thing that tends to come to our mind and out of our mouth is complaining. The truth is, all of us struggle with this at times. Carefully meditate on these passages from God's Word and allow them to soak in and renew your thinking:

   Do all things without grumbling and faultfinding and complaining [against God] and questioning and doubting [among yourselves].
   Philippians 2:14 *AMPC*

   Let your character or moral disposition be free from love of money [including greed, avarice, lust, and craving for earthly possessions] and be satisfied with your present [circumstances

and with what you have]; for He [God] Himself has said, I will not in ANY WAY fail you nor give you up nor leave you without support. [I will] not, [I will] not, [I will] not in any degree leave you helpless nor forsake nor let [you] down (relax My hold on you)! [Assuredly not!]

Hebrews 13:5 (AMPC)

3. The essence of the prayer of agreement is *unity*. When two or more believers come together in unity and agree on what God has said, great things happen! Carefully reflect on the vivid picture of unity in Psalm 133:1-3. What does God equate unity to in verses 2 and 3? And how does He respond when you get into agreement with other believers (verse 3)?

PRACTICAL APPLICATION

But be ye doers of the word, and not hearers only,
deceiving your own selves.
— James 1:22

1. The *prayer of thanksgiving* — from the word *eucharisteo* — refers to *wonderful feelings and good sentiments that freely flow up out of the heart in response to something or someone.* Who has touched your life in such a profound way that when you think of them, overwhelming appreciation wells up inside of you that you can hardly contain? What about them has so blessed your life?

2. Have you taken time to sincerely thank God for them? Why not take the next few moments to verbally express your appreciation for these precious people and pray for God's blessings to be poured out into their lives.

3. Have you ever come together with someone and prayed a prayer of agreement concerning a situation? If so, what did you ask God to do? How did He respond and answer your concert of prayer?

4. What present situation do you really need someone to agree with you about in prayer? Who can you get together with in prayer? What promise (or promises) from God's Word can you *believe in your heart* and *confess with your mouth* to God, asking Him to bring to pass?

TOPIC

Prayer of Supplication, Prayer of Intercession

SCRIPTURES

1. **Ephesians 6:18** — Praying always with all prayer and supplication in the Spirit, and watching thereunto with all perseverance and supplication for all saints.

2. **Romans 8:26** — Likewise the Spirit also helpeth our infirmities: for we know not what we should pray for as we ought: but the Spirit itself [Himself] maketh intercession for us with groanings which cannot be uttered.

3. **Ephesians 6:13** — Wherefore take unto you the whole armour of God, that ye may be able to withstand in the evil day, and having done all, to stand.

GREEK WORDS

1. "with all prayer" — διὰ πάσης προσευχῆς (*dia pases proseuches*): with all kinds of prayer

2. "intercession" — ὑπερεντυγχάνω (*huperentugchano*): found only one time in the entire New Testament, making it the rarest of the words that denote different forms of prayer; the only usage of ὑπερεντυγχάνω (*huperentugchano*) in the New Testament is found in Romans 8:26

3. "infirmities" — ἀσθένεια (*astheneia*): an all-encompassing term for all types of sickness and disease; depicts those who are weak, sick, broken, or infirmed in body, mind, emotion; it may even depict spiritual infirmity; it is indicative of infirmities of all types; it can even denote financial poverty; it refers to something that is weak, base, feeble, puny, or powerless; something that is substandard, second-rate, low-grade, or inferior

SYNOPSIS

From Genesis to Revelation, we see that *prayer* is a regular practice of all those who earnestly follow God. From the well-known patriarchs of the past like Moses, David, and Elijah, to the Spirit-filled believers of the New Testament and the present day, communicating with God through prayer continues to be a powerful privilege that enables us to see God's Kingdom come and His will to be done on earth as it is in Heaven.

Through this series, we have seen that prayer is not a "one size fits all" application. God has given us various types of prayer, and each one is like a uniquely designed tool to be used to accomplish a specific task. The right kind of prayer prayed at the right time can release a powerful manifestation of God's presence and provision in every situation we face!

The emphasis of this lesson:

The prayer of supplication is another kind of prayer found in the New Testament, and it denotes a wonderful, intimate form of prayer to God in simple, childlike faith, to freely enjoy His presence and fellowship. And one more form of prayer is the prayer of intercession, when the Holy Spirit, who possesses the fullness of God, makes "intercession" for us when we don't know how or what we should pray.

A Summary of Five Kinds of Prayer We've Examined

Just as there are many different tools in a typical tool box, God has provided us with different types of powerful prayer to fight the good fight of faith. Paul made this crystal clear in Ephesians 6:18 where he said, "Praying always with all prayer and supplication in the Spirit, and watching thereunto with all perseverance and supplication for all saints."

We have seen that the phrase "with all prayer" in Greek is *dia pases proseuches*, which means *with all kinds of prayer*. This verse could also be translated "praying always with all manner of prayer," "praying always with all kinds of prayer," or "praying always with all sorts of prayer." One scholar has translated this portion of Scripture, "Praying always with all the kinds of prayers that God has made available for you to use."

In the previous four lessons, we have examined five forms of prayer God has given to the Church:

1. **The Prayer of Consecration** – The word "consecration" is from the Greek word *proseuche* — the most common word for "prayer" in the New Testament, used 127 times. This word depicts a divine exchange in which a person comes *face to face with God* and makes a *pledge* or a *vow* in order to receive something he needs. The fact that this word appears 127 times tells us that God is calling us to regularly come to the altar and surrender our lives to Him in exchange for His life. (For a review of the *prayer of consecration*, refer back to Lesson 2.)

2. **The Prayer of Petition** – The word "petition" is a translation of the Greek word *deesis*, and it depicts one who feels he has an *urgent need* in his life that only God alone can fill. It is the picture of a believer who humbly recognizes his *utter dependence on God*, and, therefore, pleads with Him from the depths of his spirit and soul to graciously move on his behalf and meet his need — whether it be spiritual, mental, or emotional. (For a review of the *prayer of petition*, refer back to Lesson 3.)

3. **The Prayer of Authority** – This kind of prayer is derived from the Greek word *aiteo*, which means *to ask* or *to demand* something. When we allow the Word of God to permanently take up residence in our hearts, we have the ability to accurately pray in direct accordance with God's will. Thus, we can boldly demand, command, and require God to move on our behalf based on what He has already said in His Word. The *prayer of authority* — the Greek word *aiteo* — is sometimes called the *prayer of faith*, and it is used more than 80 times in the New Testament. (For a review of the *prayer of authority*, refer back to Lesson 3.)

4. **The Prayer of Thanksgiving** – The word "thanksgiving" is taken from the Greek word *eucharisteo*, and it describes a heart so full of *gratefulness* and *good feelings toward something or someone* that it cannot contain it. It is an appreciation that freely flows out of the heart in response to someone or something. This type of prayer is found particularly in the epistles of Paul, where he prays for believers in the various churches he has planted. This signifies that thanksgiving should have a dominant role in every aspect of our lives — especially when we're praying for others. Before we pray for people to change, we need to first remember how much God's grace has already transformed their lives and thank God for it. (For a review of the *prayer of thanksgiving*, refer back to Lesson 4.)

5. **The Prayer of Agreement** – Jesus talked about the   power of this prayer in Matthew 18:19, saying, "…If two of you shall agree on earth as touching any thing that they shall ask, it shall be done for them of my Father which is in heaven." The word "agree" in this verse is a translation of the Greek word *sumphoneo*, and it's where we get the word for a *symphony*. When we agree in prayer with someone and ask God to do what He has declared in His Word, it is like a sweet sounding symphony in His ears that He has promised to answer. (For a review of the *prayer of agreement*, refer back to Lesson 4.)

The Prayer of Supplication

The sixth form of prayer used in the New Testament is the *prayer of supplication*. This word "supplication" is a translation of the Greek word *enteuxis* and is a compound of the word *en* and a form of the word *tugchano*. The word *en* means *in* or *into*, and the word *tugchano* means *to happen upon*. When these two words are compounded, the new word *enteuxis* means *to fall into a situation* or *to happen into a circumstance with someone else*. This word *enteuxis* and its various forms are used only five times in the New Testament.

One of the places where the word *enteuxis* is used is in Paul's first letter to Timothy. He said, "For every creature of God is good, and nothing to be refused, if it be received with thanksgiving: For it is sanctified by the word of God and prayer" (1 Timothy 4:4,5). The word "prayer" in this passage is the Greek word *enteuxis*, and in this particular verse it is the picture of a person who is praying and supernaturally falls into a mode of prayer that is so accurate he is able to hit the spiritual bullseye when he prays.

Interestingly, the word *enteuxis* and its various forms are usually translated as the word "intercession" in the New Testament. However, *enteuxis* does not necessarily refer to intercession as most people think of intercession (i.e., prayer for other people). Instead, the word *enteuxis* carries the idea of one who comes to God in simple, childlike faith, to freely enjoy fellowship in the presence of the Lord.

In some places, it has been translated as the word "supplication." Indeed, this is the idea reflected in this word *enteuxis* — to *supplicate* with the Lord. This word was used in some classical writings to depict a love relationship between two lovers — two individuals who had *happened upon each other* (who had found or discovered each other) and now were sharing their lives together.

One expositor has said that *enteuxis* — the prayer of supplication — is prayer in its most individual and simple form. It literally means *to fall into* or *to happen upon*, and the idea is to *fall into the presence of the Lord* or *to come into wonderful relationship in prayer*.

This word *enteuxis* denotes a wonderful, intimate form of prayer whereby we learn to come before God in childlike faith to freely express ourselves and our desires and to unreservedly enjoy His wonderful presence. Furthermore, the prayer of supplication refers to those special times in prayer when God by His Spirit showers us in love and fills us with the knowledge of His life-transforming acceptance. Thank God for the glorious privilege He has extended to us to enjoy this kind of intimate fellowship with Him!

The Prayer of Intercession

There is one more very rare form of prayer featured in the New Testament, and it is the *prayer of intercession*. It is taken from the Greek word *huperentugchano*, a word found only one time in the entire New Testament, making it the rarest of the words that denote different forms of prayer. In fact, it is so unique, its appearance in Scripture is the first time chronologically it is used in any piece of literature, which means when the verse was written, the Holy Spirit coined a word that had never been used anywhere else to describe His supernatural help.

The only usage of the word *huperentugchano* is found in Romans 8:26, and it is translated as "intercession." This verse says:

> **Likewise the Spirit also helpeth our infirmities: for we know not what we should pray for as we ought: but the Spirit itself [Himself] maketh intercession for us with groanings which cannot be uttered.**

In this verse, we see it is the divine presence of the Holy Spirit Himself who is doing the praying. Think about it. The magnificent Third Person of the Trinity who possesses the fullness of God is making "intercession" for us when we don't know how or what we should pray. He is literally *falling in on our behalf* to help us when we cannot help ourselves.

There is something very unique about this word "intercession" — the Greek word *huperentugchano*. It is what we would call a word for *rescue*. For instance, if someone fell deep into a cavern, you would have to descend down into that cavern along with that person in order to get him out and rescue him. By using this word in Romans 8:26, Paul describes those times when the Spirit of God supernaturally joins us in our circumstances, shares our emotions and frustrations, and then begins working a plan that will ultimately get each of us out of that troublesome mess!

Suddenly and supernaturally, the Holy Spirit falls into that place of helplessness and joins with you in the rhythm of prayer. With all His wonderful attributes and personality traits, the Spirit still feels everything you feel. He empathizes with your feelings of complete inadequacy. He understands the battles you are facing. He willingly falls into each difficult circumstance along with you, feeling your emotions of fear, anger, or frustration. Then He begins a plan of rescue! That is the purpose of the prayer of intercession — it is so you can be rescued, renewed, and delivered from the predicament you're facing.

What Is the Holy Spirit Rescuing Us Out of?

Notice that Paul said, "…The Spirit also helpeth our infirmities…" (Romans 8:26). The word "infirmities" in Greek is the word *astheneia*, which is an all-encompassing term for *all types of sickness and disease*. It depicts those who are *weak, sick, broken*, or *infirmed in body, mind, and emotion*. It may even depict spiritual infirmity. Furthermore, it is indicative of infirmities of all types and can even denote financial poverty. It refers to something that is weak, base, feeble, puny, or powerless; something that is substandard, second-rate, low-grade, or inferior.

What's unique about Romans 8:26 is that if you read just a little bit further, Paul identifies the greatest "infirmity" we possess. He said, "…For we know not what we should pray for as we ought.…" The word "what" is the Greek word *tis*, and it describes *the most minute, minuscule detail*. Paul's use of this word is the equivalent of him saying, "We often don't even know how to pray accurately about the smallest, most minute details of our lives."

Then he adds the word "ought" — we don't know how to pray as we "ought." This word "ought" in Greek is the word *de*, and it describes *an obligation* or *a necessity*. Therefore, you could translate this part of the verse to say, "We do not know how to pray as every new circumstance requires." This indicates that there is no general formula of prayer that you can pray for every situation. Each new circumstance is going to require a brand new, specific kind of prayer.

For instance, let's say you or someone you love is battling sickness, and it has been going on for quite some time. You know from your general knowledge of God's Word that it is His will to heal. However, you don't know how to specifically release God's healing power into the person who desperately needs it. This is where the Holy Spirit is ready to fall into where you are and make intercession for you.

There is only one Person who knows how to pray accurately in every situation you face, and that is the Holy Spirit. He knows everything about everything — past, present, and future. Not only does He know the root cause of every problem and infirmity, He also knows the specific will of God for every person that will ever live. So if we try to pray *without* the Holy Spirit's help, our efforts will always be futile. We simply don't have the know-how apart from Him.

To get results from our prayers, we must recognize our own human weakness and total dependence on God. This will begin to open our hearts and souls to this intercessory ministry of the Holy Spirit. The moment we come to grips with our need for supernatural assistance and cry out for the Holy Spirit's help, we liberate Him to release His power on the inside of us. As we humble ourselves and ask for the Spirit's help, He will pray through us and get results!

A Final Word

Friend, no matter what challenge you encounter, your ultimate victory depends on whether or not you use the prayer tools God has provided for you. Therefore, if you want to live as more than a conqueror in this life, embrace these anointed words of instruction from Paul:

> **Wherefore take unto you the whole armour of God, that ye may be able to withstand in the evil day, and having done all, to stand.**
> **Ephesians 6:13**

Remember, part of your armor is the *lance of prayer*. Paul said you are to be "praying always with all prayer and supplication in the Spirit..." (Ephesians 6:18). This means...

Anytime you get a chance, no matter where you are or what you are doing, at every opportunity, every season, and every possible moment — SEIZE that time to pray!

STUDY QUESTIONS

> Study to shew thyself approved unto God, a workman that needeth
> not to be ashamed, rightly dividing the word of truth.
> — 2 Timothy 2:15

1. Of all the different kinds of prayer presented in these five lessons, which one are you most familiar with and have used most often? Which kind of prayer is least familiar, but you have a strong desire to learn more about?

2. The idea of the *prayer of supplication* is to fall into the presence of the Lord or to come into wonderful relationship with Him in prayer. Have you experienced a special time in prayer like this — when God by His Spirit showered you in *love* and filled you with the knowledge of His life-transforming acceptance? Consider Paul's prayer in Ephesians 3:14-19 and make it a personalized prayer of your own.

3. One question that many people have is, "Why do my prayers sometimes not get answered?" Although we cannot identify every reason, the Bible does reveal some common causes for unanswered prayer. Read the following verses and identify these reasons.

    • **Psalm 66:18**

    • **Proverbs 1:28-31; 28:9**

    • **Isaiah 1:15-19**

    • **Isaiah 59:1-3 and Micah 3:4**

    • **James 1:6-8**

    • **James 4:2,3**

    What is the Holy Spirit speaking to you personally as you read through these passages?

PRACTICAL APPLICATION

But be ye doers of the word, and not hearers only,
deceiving your own selves.
— James 1:22

1. The *prayer of supplication* is when a person supernaturally falls into a mode of prayer that is so accurate he is able to hit the spiritual bullseye when he prays. Have you ever prayed this type of prayer for someone? If so, describe how God moved on you to pray and what supernatural events took place as a result.

2. Have you ever been the recipient of someone praying a *prayer of supplication* for you? Describe what took place when they came alongside you in that difficult situation and earnestly prayed to God for His intervention in your life.

3. Can you recall a time when the Holy Spirit Himself prayed the *prayer of intercession* through you — a time when He joined you in your circumstances, shared your emotions and frustrations, and began working a plan that ultimately rescued you out of the mess you were in? Briefly explain what took place.

4. The *prayer of intercession* by the Holy Spirit rescues us out of "infirmities," which describes *all types of sickness and disease* and depicts those who are *weak, sick, broken*, or *infirmed in body, mind, and emotion*. What "infirmities" are you currently facing that you need the Holy Spirit to rescue you out of?

5. To receive the matchless intercessory ministry of the Holy Spirit, you must first recognize your own human weakness and total dependence on God. Don't let pride prevent you from receiving the supernatural help of the Holy Spirit. *Humble yourself* and ask the Lord to forgive you of being prideful in any way and to move into action on your behalf.

Notes

Notes

_____
_____
_____
_____
_____
_____
_____
_____
_____
_____
_____
_____
_____
_____
_____
_____
_____
_____
_____
_____
_____
_____
_____
_____
_____
_____
_____
_____
_____
_____
_____
_____

Notes

Notes

_____
_____
_____
_____
_____
_____
_____
_____
_____
_____
_____
_____
_____
_____
_____
_____
_____
_____
_____
_____
_____
_____
_____
_____
_____
_____
_____
_____

Notes